WHILE YOU WAIT
ACTIVATING YOUR FAITH

A 7-DAY DEVOTIONAL JOURNAL

Tomeria Jordan

Confident Connotations Publishing

While You Wait - Activating Your Faith
A 7-Day Devotional Journal

© 2021-2023 Tomeria Jordan

All Rights Reserved.

Editors (2021): Amber Ivey and Meron Seife

Confident Connotations Publishing
ISBN: 979-8-9887040-1-0
For Worldwide Distribution

CONTENTS

Foreword

I dedicate this book to my late Great-Grandmother Corine Allen, who is a pillar of faith in my life. She has always had faith in God and exemplified unconditional love every day. That faith was most evident during one my most memorable life-changing events, an F4 tornado.

On August 6, 1993 at approximately 1:30PM, our lives were turned upside down by a tornado moving at 30 miles per hour with top wind speeds of 210 miles per hour. With no forewarning, we found ourselves scrambling to take shelter within my grandmother's home. As the wind was howling, the home began violently shaking but she was not shaken. In the middle of my terrifying screams and tears my great-grandmother encouraged me, my aunt, and cousin to "be quiet, be still." After the shaking ended there was an eerie silence.

Upon walking outside of the house and seeing all the devastation surrounding us we knew that nothing would be the same.

As I navigate life, now more than ever, Corine's words still ring true and I can hear her whispering to me during life's storms to "be quiet, be still."

Granny, as she was so affectionately called, remained calm for the 96 years God blessed her to be on this earth and never seemed to allow worry to overtake her because she had faith that God would work everything out for our good. Granny's strength is to be admired and her love for family, friends and neighbors adored. To my lifelong angel, your mark on my life and this world will live on. Because God blessed you, we are here still standing strong and standing proud.

In this moment of your life, I encourage you to "be quiet, be still" and know that God knows what you need. Over the next seven days may your faith be activated as you spend more time with God, find your inner strength, and reflect on where you've been, where you are, and raise your level of expectation for where you are going.

Day 1: Faith Over Fear

"Now faith is confidence in what we hope for and assurance about what we do not see."

Hebrews 11:1

In today's world we are plagued by images that instill fear, worry, doubt, and frustration. This fear triggers feelings of despair, defeat, and depression. It is natural and quite common to fear the unknown or that which we do not understand because I have experienced this firsthand. The tornado that ravaged my neighborhood created fear for me, my family, friends, and neighbors. Now let's take a trip down memory lane.

It was a warm summer day, and we were in the middle of an English lesson. Me and the rest of the fourth graders were attentively completing ad libs with the recent list of vocabulary terms that we had just learned. Within what seemed like a few minutes the sky turned dark. It was a very ominous sight, and I immediately went from an engaged student to terrified. I jumped under the desk as an announcement came across the intercom requesting all students take shelter. My teacher tried to usher me out of the classroom with the other students, but I would not budge. I was literally overtaken with fear. Some of my classmates laughed, others were also afraid, and some were just as concerned as my teacher that I would not move. I was crying hysterically and shaking because this looked all too familiar. After about 10 minutes the storm was moving in, the lightning was flashing, and the rolling thunder began. I finally gave in and left the classroom with my teacher who assured me we would be safer with the rest of the students in the gymnasium.

In this instance, I went from enjoying what I was doing to being bound by fear. Fear and faith are like oil and water; they do not mix. The only exception to this rule is revering the Lord.

Fear of what happens on earth stops us in our tracks and makes us stagnant; however, faith allows us to keep moving no matter the situation, test, or trial. So, what is faith? The bible indicates that it is "confidence in what we hope for and assurance about what we do not see." This simply means we must confidently trust that what we are believing in will come to pass. Believe that you will see better days, improved situations, changing circumstances, and outcomes.

Exercising our faith muscle makes it easier to bear the weight of the wait. Whatever you are waiting for, or hoping for, take courage in knowing that the best is yet to come. This hopeful expectation is what gives you a different perspective and helps you enjoy the journey. Regardless of what life situations look like we can stand on God's word that promises he will never leave or forsake us, but we must believe and not doubt.

<u>While You Wait Principle</u>

Acknowledge when you are feeling fearful yet remember you can choose to forge ahead.

REFLECTION

_____

_____

_____

_____

_____

_____

_____

_____

_____

_____

_____

_____

_____

_____

_____

_____

_____

_____

_____

_____

_____

_____

_____

_____

_____

_____

_____

_____

_____

_____

_____

_____

_____

_____

_____

_____

_____

_____

_____

_____

_____

_____

_____

_____

Day 2: Watch Your Mouth

"The tongue has the power of life and death, and those who love it will eat its fruit."

Proverbs 18:21

Throughout my life I have realized the power of words and labels. Words have the power to send us in a tailspin if we aren't careful. In fact, I've seen this lesson play out time and time again in different capacities. For instance, since I was younger, I always heard that I was "big." To put this in context, I was tall for my age and curvy. Back then I struggled with self-esteem because I heard I was "big" so often I thought that I was. Fast forward to now when I look back at pictures, I wish I was that size. Because I received and believed that I was "big" I gained weight and struggled with my self-esteem for many years even into adulthood.

It is amazing how what we say manifests itself in our lives. I now realize that I have haphazardly spoken things over myself, and I've allowed others to speak over me in a manner that is not always conducive to God's will for my life.

When we fail to speak positively about the situations in our lives, we confine ourselves to the negative thoughts and opinions that stifle purpose and hinders God from moving. It's not that God can't, it's just that God loves us so much that we are given the ability to choose.

In Proverbs 18:21, we are reminded that the power of life and death are in the tongue, and we will eat the fruit (outcomes). Watching what I say was and is sometimes still a struggle for me because we are human; however, our Savior redeems and can help us grow in this area. If we are thirsty, he will give us a drink. If we hunger for righteousness, he will surely feed us. It may not look like what we expect but his word cannot and will not return to him void. What we put out into the world manifests itself. If we speak love, we will see and receive love. Similarly, if we spew hate we get the same in return.

Because you are worth it, let go of negativity! Of course, this is easier said than done. In fact, it's like committing to a workout schedule or diet. For some, this comes easy. For others this is a daunting task. Why? Like a diet or choosing to exercise, it's a choice! Once you build the habit you will question why you didn't do it sooner. Akin to working out, let's exercise our positivity muscle so that no good thing will be withheld from us. What we believe, we say. What we say, we do.

While You Wait Principle

What you say is as powerful as what you believe. From the heart, the mouth speaks.

TOMERIA JORDAN

REFLECTION

_____

_____

_____

_____

_____

_____

_____

_____

_____

_____

_____

_____

_____

_____

_____

_____

_____

_____

_____

_____

_____

_____

_____

_____

_____

_____

_____

_____

_____

_____

_____

_____

_____

_____

_____

_____

_____

_____

_____

_____

_____

_____

_____

_____

Day 3: Mind-Full

"Above all else, guard your heart, for everything you do flows from it."

Proverbs 4:23

For close to 30 years of my life I would watch the news in the morning, evening, and before bed. When I reflect on this time, I have come to realize that the constant barrage of bad news made me feel afraid, anxious, and worried more often than I felt peace. In fact, when I think back to the time immediately following the tornado on August 6, 1993, I would literally sit in front of the TV for hours watching weather updates, especially on days in which the sky presented more ominously. This obsession became evident in a conversation with a therapist who shared how our perspectives in life are shaped not only by our experiences but what we see and hear.

I've heard people say, "think about what you're thinking about." I believe this means considering your thoughts and the impact they have on your life and overall spiritual wellbeing. In the last few years, I've started to make a more concerted effort to guard my heart by being mindful of what I watch and/or allow to consume my mind. There are so many images that we allow to permeate our souls and unless it's life giving, we are dying a slow death inside. Sometimes wishing, hoping, and praying for freedom that will only come by acknowledging the power of our thoughts, social circles, societal influences, and media.

Today, consider your heart's true condition. What are you thinking about, talking about, or hearing? Are your thoughts or conversations helpful or harmful? Whatever your personal inventory reveals, make a conscious decision to seek God for clarity and guidance on the actions you should take to move forward in faith.

<u>While You Wait Principle</u>

Allow the Holy Spirit to guide you in
Spirit and in truth, helping you see clearly
what and who to open your heart to.

REFLECTION

_____

_____

_____

_____

_____

_____

_____

_____

_____

_____

_____

_____

_____

_____

_____

_____

_____

_____

_____

_____

_____

_____

_____

_____

_____

_____

_____

_____

TOMERIA JORDAN

_____

_____

_____

_____

_____

_____

_____

_____

_____

_____

_____

_____

_____

_____

_____

Day 4: Don't Doubt, Do

"What good is it, my brothers and sisters, if someone claims to have faith but has no deeds? Can such faith save them?"

James 2:14

In our walk of faith, it is easy to hope for things without taking the necessary action to achieve the goal. Imagine looking for a job, hoping you will get one, yet never taking the time to apply. I can say there have been times in my life where I let fear stop me from applying for a job because I didn't believe I met all the qualifications. Working across various industries for the past 25 years I now know that sometimes the age-old cliché is true, "it's not what you know, it's who you know." Not to mention recognizing that in some instances there are individuals less qualified doing the job we may want to do but we weren't willing to walk in faith and apply. The Word tells us plainly in James 2:26 that "faith without works is dead."

In James 2, two vivid examples underline the inseparable link between faith and action. The first centers around

Abraham's willingness to offer his son Isaac as a sacrifice, showcasing how his faith was manifested through his obedience. "Abraham believed God, and it was credited to him as righteousness," and he was called God's friend." The second example highlights Rahab, the prostitute, who, by aiding the spies and protecting them, demonstrated her faith through her courageous deeds. In both cases, James emphasizes that genuine faith is not a passive concept; rather, it finds its full expression through tangible actions that validate its authenticity.

Whatever you are believing God for today ask and believe that God will give you wisdom through the power of the Holy Spirit so that you can take the necessary steps to activate your faith. Some steps may be more straightforward, like filling out an application for a job whereas others may require you to fast and pray for guidance depending on the situation. Either way, your belief requires action so don't be afraid to take the first step. Often, I've found the first step is the key to unlocking your true potential.

<u>While You Wait Principle</u>

Faith and action work together!

REFLECTION

_____

_____

_____

_____

_____

_____

_____

_____

_____

_____

_____

_____

_____

_____

_____

_____

_____

_____

_____

_____

_____

_____

_____

_____

_____

_____

_____

_____

_____

_____

_____

_____

_____

_____

_____

_____

_____

_____

_____

_____

_____

_____

_____

_____

_____

Day 5: Hold Steady

"Let us hold unswervingly to the hope
we profess, for he who promised is
faithful."

Hebrews 10:23

For years I struggled with comparison and didn't understand why some people seemingly got away with some things whereas I felt that I was held to a much higher standard. At times it was frustrating because I didn't understand how individuals who openly bragged about not having the same standard set for them could skate by. Initially it would frustrate me because I would go above and beyond only to be told it wasn't good enough, yet I would witness others submit average work and be praised.

Similarly, when it comes to spiritual convictions, I felt like I would get convicted often when trying to live in the world's system, following societal norms, and giving in to temptation, and sin. Yet I'd see other believers who felt like it was okay to sin because God's grace and forgiveness would cover us. After all, this is what many

Christians have seen, people engaging in sinful behaviors and when they have matured in age, they turn their life around.

The misconception about sin today is when we see others thriving in sin, we start to believe there will be no consequences for our actions. We may feel more inclined to push the boundaries, moving beyond our spiritual convictions.

Matthew 5:45 reminds us that it rains on the just and the unjust. As a result, comparing our lives to others can put us in a dangerous position especially when we begin to operate outside of wisdom and Godly convictions. Because God is omniscient, attempting to understand what we see in the natural is like trying to compare 3rd-grade math to trigonometry. It just doesn't add up. God looks at our heart and not our outward appearances. God forgives yet it is not wise to continue to test the bounds of God's grace because the Word also reminds us that we reap what we sow.

Therefore, we should ask God to help us remember that everything can work together for our good regardless of how difficult the situation may seem. When we think about Jesus, he is the "pioneer and perfecter of faith." (Hebrews 12:2) In fact, his faith is why we have 2nd, 3rd, 4th or more chances to get it right. His sacrifice on the cross covers our sin but we must hold steady in faith to trust that God can deliver us from any situation and that includes comparison and the strength to turn away from sin. Sin often hinders our ability to believe because we know that it separates us from God. With faith in Jesus, we understand that we can be saved by believing in our hearts and confessing with our mouths that Jesus is Lord.

So, whenever you feel like giving up, and think that what you do doesn't matter it is important to remember that every day may not be easy but in the end it's worth it to hold steady in faith.

<u>While You Wait Principle</u>

Maintaining faith amid life's raging storms creates the catalyst you need to move from glory to glory. Every valley isn't a pit and mountains vary in size and shape.

REFLECTION

_____

_____

_____

_____

_____

_____

_____

_____

_____

_____

_____

_____

_____

_____

_____

_____

_____

_____

_____

_____

_____

_____

_____

_____

_____

_____

_____

_____

_____

Day 6: He Reigns

"…according to his eternal purpose that
he accomplished in Christ Jesus our Lord.
In him and through faith in him we may
approach God with freedom and
confidence."

Ephesians 3:11-12

On a profound Friday, November 16, 2018, a pivotal chapter in my life unfolded – the same life chapter to which this book is devoted. My incredible great-grandmother, Corine, affectionately known as Granny, suffered a monumental stroke, and the medical consensus was grim: life support was the only thread connecting her to us. It's etched in my memory how I wept into my pillow that night, heart heavy with prayers. As dawn broke, I urgently phoned my grandmother, Dorothy, who shared that, miraculously, Granny was still breathing, detached from the ventilator. Though not fully conscious, her breath remained a resolute testament to the incredible interplay of faith and grace. This illuminated for me that against earthly odds, God's merciful hand sustained her existence until an unforgettable Sunday, November 18th. This window of grace allowed me and our extended family members who weren't in town the sacred opportunity to bid her farewell. Like the instance on August 6, 1993, when she whispered to me, my cousin, and my aunt, "be quiet, be still," she clung to her faith in God's timing until He beckoned her home.

Jesus grants us direct access to God if we are willing to repent of our sins and confess that Jesus is Lord. Much like salvation, we often forget that our faith requires specific actions to help us achieve God's will for our lives. When we combine our beliefs with action it changes our perspective and permits us to move forward to complete whatever task is before us. In Ephesians 3:20 it notes that Jesus' power lives within us, which is the power that permits us to do much more than we can ask or imagine.

All of God's children have an inheritance

that is unmatched by anything we can see in the physical. When you start to feel anxiety grow, speak to those negative spirits, and cast them down in the name of Jesus where they belong. Under your feet! Because Jesus lives, we can ask and believe in faith that God's word will not return to Him void. "Whatever happens, conduct yourselves in a manner worthy of the gospel of Christ. Then, whether I come and see you or only hear about you in my absence, I will know that you stand firm in the one Spirit, striving together as one for the faith of the gospel." (Philippians 1:27)

While You Wait Principle

Stand in faith knowing that we have the
same spirit within us that raised Jesus
from the dead, allowing him to conquer
death and the grave.

TOMERIA JORDAN

REFLECTION

_____

_____

_____

_____

_____

_____

_____

_____

_____

_____

_____

_____

_____

_____

_____

_____

_____

_____

_____

_____

_____

_____

_____

_____

_____

_____

_____

_____

_____

Day 7: Wings of Faith

"Therefore I tell you, do not worry about your life, what you will eat or drink; or about your body, what you will wear. Is not life more than food, and the body more than clothes? Look at the birds of the air; they do not sow or reap or store away in barns, and yet your heavenly Father feeds them. Are you not much more valuable than they? Can any one of you by worrying add a single hour to your life?"

Matthew 6:25-27

Life's adversities can challenge our positivity, yet with unshakable faith, triumph becomes our reality. The year 2020 dawned with a revelation of new life, as I learned of my pregnancy with our second child. But February introduced a heart-wrenching twist - a missed miscarriage, shattering our hopes as we discovered our baby's heartbeat had stilled. Hard choices were before us: allow nature's course or embrace a procedure to ease the risks. What followed was a whirlwind of fears, medical interventions, and a daunting dance with uncertainty. Despite the fear, much like the resilience shown after the unexpected tornado on August 6th, I persisted, standing stronger than ever before, held up by an unseen hand.

Amid tumultuous moments like the stories that have been shared, I birthed a vision in 2010 that is now growing and flying on the wings of faith. On March 31, 2020, amid the Covid-19 global pandemic starting the CC: America Podcast took flight, an endeavor rooted in Confidence Centers of America. It became a haven for my own faith journey, a platform where I shared stories of transformation and inspiration, igniting the sparks of faith in others. In the year that followed, I renamed the CC: America Podcast to "Confidence Restored," encapsulating the essence of my life's narrative. It's a narrative of belief, tested faith, and the wondrous restoration through the unfailing power of Jesus Christ.

Amidst the creative journey of writing and podcasting, I've encountered blessings beyond measure. My identity is blossoming, my faith in Christ has been renewed, and my spiritual strength is reaching soaring heights. These experiences illuminated the ease with which we can succumb to stagnation, resting within the comfort of where we are. But, as with the dawn after rest, arises the imperative to rise, to forge ahead.

Contemplate the wisdom of birds as they learn to fly. They trust their wings, knowing they are equipped for flight. Parallel to this, do you have faith in your wings — the aspirations that propel you? This is a question only you can answer.

Remember, desires and dreams are deserving of immediate pursuit. Proverbs 18:16 reinforces that our gifts make way for us. Embrace the Holy Spirit's whisper, moving with its guidance. Emerge when the time is ripe or linger in stillness until your spirit signals release. Within the kingdom of God, each of us is entrusted with a unique role, a responsibility not to be taken lightly. It is a responsibility to honor God, to honor ourselves, and to honor others.

Let this chapter remind you that adversity, though a formidable force, cannot extinguish the flame of faith. Raise your gaze, spread your wings, and venture forward. For within you lies the potential to rise, to inspire, and to fulfill a destiny woven into the tapestry of a grander design.

While You Wait Principle

Embrace the freedom of faith!

REFLECTION

_____

_____

_____

_____

_____

_____

_____

_____

_____

_____

_____

_____

_____

_____

_____

_____

_____

_____

_____

_____

_____

_____

_____

_____

_____

_____

_____

_____

_____

_____

_____

_____

_____

_____

_____

_____

_____

_____

_____

_____

_____

_____

_____

Acknowledgements

All praise, glory, and honor to God for giving me the vision to inspire the lives of others through service, dedication, and faith over a decade ago. This process of transformation has been immensely valuable. Through highs and lows, I can honestly say at the time that I began this book and finished it, I am grateful for every life experience, both good and bad. Each experience taught me valuable lessons and provided clarity which is allowing me to move forward in faith to fulfill what I believe is my God ordained destiny.

To my husband, Rodney, and my daughter, Nadia, your presence in my life has been a blessing yet has challenged me in unexpected ways. While none of us know what the future holds, I am motivated and believe that everything will work together for our good. My faith in what is,

The Confidence Restored Podcast

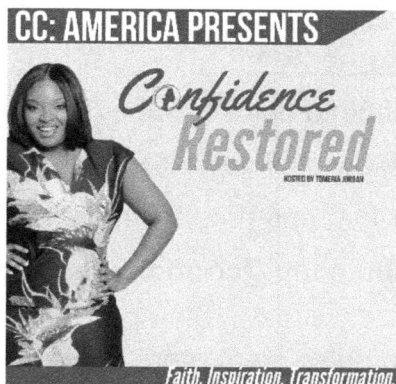

CC: America presents the Confidence Restored Podcast hosted by Tomeria Jordan. This is a show designed to help you build your confidence, increase your faith, and get mentally FIT to overcome any trials and tribulations you may encounter. Through personal testimonies of Faith, Inspiration, and Transformation, Tomeria and guests seek to inspire and uplift you. This message is delivered by us CC'ing you on lessons learned in hopes of encouraging you regardless of where you are in life. Let's get FIT together.

Get Connected!

Subscribe to our YouTube Channel for available visual podcast episodes, more inspiration, and entertainment. **youtube.com/@confidencerestored**.

You can also learn more or access audio podcast links via **confidencerestoredpodcast.com** or **linktr.ee/ccamericallc**.

About The Author

Tomeria Jordan is a passionate author, speaker, and thought leader dedicated to inspiring individuals to live with confidence, purpose, and faith. With over 25 years of experience across various industries, Tomeria brings a wealth of knowledge and expertise to her writing. She holds a master's degree in learning and performance technology from the University of Maryland, Baltimore County, and a bachelor's degree in international business and economics from Old Dominion University. With her inspiring messages, Tomeria Jordan is committed to helping individuals discover their true potential, find healing and restoration, and live a purposeful and confident life.

Pocahontas Island

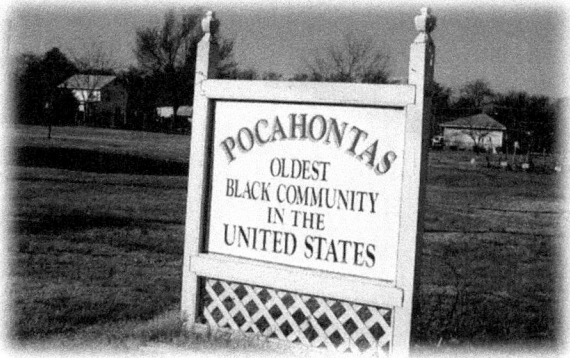

Pocahontas Island is a nationally registered historical landmark and is the place me and many of my family members call home. Pocahontas Island is noted as the "Oldest Black Community in the United States" with evidence that this island was previously an Indigenous American settlement. I encourage you to research Pocahontas Island when you have some time, we have a deep and rich history that is so vast it's hard to define.

www.ingramcontent.com/pod-product-compliance
Lightning Source LLC
Chambersburg PA
CBHW060344050426
42449CB00011B/2826